Heartfelt Holidays

Devotionals for Thanksgiving & Christmas

Kelly Wenner

www.soulstrengthfit.com

Contents

Welcome to Heartfelt Holidays

Devotionals for Thanksgiving & Christmas

Reflect, Rejoice, and Renew Your Spirit this Holiday Season

The holiday season is often filled with a flurry of activities, to-do lists, and gatherings that can quickly sweep us away from the true heart of Thanksgiving and Christmas. Yet, it's during this busy time of year that we most need a daily moment to pause, ground ourselves in God's Word, and remember the true purpose of this season. This book of devotionals is designed to be your daily anchor—a simple, impactful way to maintain a heart of gratitude, joy, and peace amid all the season's busyness.

In each day's reading, you'll have the opportunity to slow down, reflect, and deepen your connection with God. You'll engage in scripture, meditate on His promises, and take small steps toward living out the love, hope, and joy that Christ brings to the world. Through these devotionals, you're invited to approach this season with renewed focus, finding purpose and calm in the midst of chaos, and reconnecting with the spirit of gratitude that Thanksgiving and Christmas inspire.

For an enriched experience that nurtures both body and soul, consider pairing these devotionals with the *Giving Thanks* and *The 12 Workouts of Christmas* programs from SoulStrength Fit. These programs include faith-centered workouts that complement the devotionals, creating a holistic experience that nurtures both body and soul. Visit www.soulstrengthfit.com to learn more.

May this journey through the holiday season bring you closer to Christ, helping you celebrate His love, cultivate gratitude, and experience the fullness of joy He offers.

The Heart of Thanksgiving

A Week of Grateful Reflection

Day 1: The Heart of Thanksgiving

Gratitude is a doorway into God's presence. Begin by reading Psalm 100.

"Enter His gates with thanksgiving." Thanksgiving is how we are to enter into God's presence. If you ever find yourself wishing you could hear God's voice more clearly or feel His presence more deeply, perhaps the problem is you haven't entered through His gates. Although we may come to God with tears, needs, or even complaints, we experience Him most intimately when we first enter with thanksgiving. Once you've entered, you can bring your requests before Him, but start with a heart of gratitude and praise.

Consider making thanksgiving a habit at the beginning of each prayer and at the start of every day. Notice the difference it makes in how you sense His presence and how clearly you hear His voice.

Take a moment now to enter God's presence with thanksgiving. What can you lift up to Him in gratitude right now? Name three specific things:

One common struggle we may share is ingratitude. With so much at our disposal, we often lose our sense of gratitude and dependence on God. Ingratitude can hinder our generosity toward others, whether financially, through patience, forgiveness, compassion, or Christ-like love. It also robs us of humility and brings a sense of dissatisfaction into our lives.

Psalm 100 provides seven ways to praise—ways to cultivate a spirit of thanksgiving:

1. **Make a joyful shout to the Lord** (v.1). Use your voice! When God does something good and powerful in your life, get vocal and shout some words of praise! It may not be in the grocery store, but perhaps in the car, on a walk, or with your family. God loves to hear our shouts of joy!

2. **Worship and serve with gladness** (v.2). Worship in church, during quiet devotional time, or even during a SoulStrength Fit workout. Worship can be expressed in our actions—using our energy, time, and strength as an offering to God. "Therefore, I urge you, brothers and sisters, in view of God's mercy, to offer your bodies as a living sacrifice, holy and pleasing to God—this is your true and proper worship." (Romans 12:1)

3. **Come into His presence with singing** (v.2). Don't worry about having a perfect voice; God delights in your songs. Whether in the car, the shower, or while doing chores, let your worship songs express the gratitude in your heart.

4. **Know that the Lord is God** (v.3). True worship is grounded in truth. To worship God fully, know who He is, what He has done, and who you are in Him. Spend time in His Word and prayer. Seek God, and you will find Him.

5. **Enter His gates with thanksgiving** (v.4). Approach God in prayer with a heart full of gratitude.

Thanksgiving not only brings us closer to His presence, but it also enhances our peace and joy.

6. **Give Him thanks** (v.4). *"Every good and perfect gift is from above, coming down from the Father of the heavenly lights."* God is the source of all goodness. Throughout your day, remember to thank Him.

7. **Praise His name** (v.4). When we praise His name, we acknowledge all that He is. We praise Him for His goodness, His enduring love, and His faithfulness to His promises. *"For the Lord is good and His love endures forever; His faithfulness continues through all generations."* (Psalm 100:5)

Psalm 100 is a powerful call to gratitude and praise. Reading it alone isn't enough to bring lasting change; we must be deliberate in our praise and build the habit of beginning our prayers with thanksgiving. As you make thanksgiving a part of your daily routine, a grateful heart will begin to feel natural.

Read Psalm 100 one more time. Of these seven ways to praise, which one will you put into practice today?

Day 2: Maintaining a Thankful Heart

Read: Philippians 4:4-7

How are you doing with not being anxious about anything?
"Do not be anxious about anything, but in every situation, by prayer and petition, with thanksgiving, present your requests to God." This verse can be challenging to live out. Not being anxious at all? For many of us, that sounds impossible. Yet, alongside our requests, we're told to always include thanksgiving. Often, our prayer life centers around our needs and pleas for help, but God invites us to bring our prayers *with* thanksgiving.

Take a moment to reflect on your current requests and pair them with gratitude. First write your current prayer requests, and then write how you can specifically show thankfulness as you lift that request to the Lord.

Prayers and Petitions

With Thanksgiving

_____

_____

_____

There is a wonderful power in the "formula" laid out in this verse. First, we're encouraged to pray at all times—starting our day, during breakfast, driving, working, exercising… In every part of your day, invite God into your life. His presence brings peace and joy. Adding thanksgiving into these interactions with the Lord will transform your mindset! Imagine if, through each moment of your day, you acknowledged and thanked God for His blessings. It would shift your focus from problems and worries to the goodness and faithfulness of God.

Read: Colossians 3:12-17

What characteristics does this passage describe that believers should embody?

Which of these characteristics do you find most challenging to embody or need to focus on more in your daily life?

In verses 15-17, we see how gratitude and worship go hand in hand. A grateful heart upholds true worship, ready to rejoice in God's goodness and offer Him praise.

Often, however, instead of hearts filled with thanksgiving, our minds can be controlled by fear. Pastor Craig Groeschel outlines four common fears:

- **The fear of loss.** This fear might include the loss of family, marriage, finances, or even youthful health.
- **The fear of failure.** This can keep people from pursuing dreams, going back to school, trying something new, or setting goals.
- **The fear of rejection.** Fear of rejection keeps people from forming relationships or leads to walls that hinder deep connection.
- **The fear of the unknown.** This fear is like a dread about what's coming next or the worry of all that could go wrong.

Which of these fears resonates with you? How does it show up in your life?

"For God has not given us a spirit of fear, but of power and of love and of a sound mind." —2 Timothy 1:7

God does not intend for us to live ruled by fear and anxiety. Instead, He calls us to lives of peace, joy, gratitude, and love. Spend some quiet moments with the Lord. Offer Him your thanksgiving and praise. Ask where He may be calling you to lay down your fears and cultivate a deeper spirit of gratitude.

Day 3: My Gratitude is a Blessing to Others

What are three things you are thankful for today?

Gratitude is a daily choice. Paul and Silas were two disciples who set out to fulfill Jesus' call by boldly sharing the message of Christ and praying for others. But because of their obedience, they faced hardship: beaten, arrested, and thrown into prison. Despite their circumstances, they chose to praise God instead of giving in to discouragement or bitterness.

Read: Acts 16:22-26

"A mob quickly formed against Paul and Silas, and the city officials ordered them stripped and beaten with wooden rods. They were severely beaten, and then they were thrown into prison. The jailer was ordered to make sure they didn't escape. So the jailer put them into the inner dungeon and clamped their feet in the stocks.
Around midnight Paul and Silas were praying and singing hymns to God, and the other prisoners were listening. Suddenly, there was a massive earthquake, and the prison was shaken to its foundations. All the doors immediately flew open, and the chains of every prisoner fell off!"

What an amazing example of how, while we may not always be able to control our circumstances, we can control our response. Paul and Silas chose an attitude of gratitude. Even though they were suffering, uncertain, and in physical pain, they decided to maintain a spirit of thanksgiving and praise.

When was the last time you felt mistreated or hurt by someone? How did you respond? What differences do you see between your response and that of Paul and Silas?

It's amazing to note that Paul and Silas's ability to respond to their imprisonment with thanksgiving not only led to their release but also profoundly impacted everyone around them. When their chains came off, "the chains of every prisoner fell off" as well. Witnessing this, the Philippian jailer sought the very salvation that Paul and Silas had been praying and singing about. The impact didn't stop there; the jailer found salvation, and so did his entire household. Filled with joy from his newfound faith, the jailer cared for Paul and Silas, washing their wounds and offering them hospitality. Paul and Silas's gratitude had spread, transforming this diligent jailer into a grateful believer.

When you choose an attitude of thanksgiving, it affects not only you but also those around you. How do you think others are impacted when you maintain an attitude of gratitude? Be specific.

Close your time in prayer. In what situations, and with which people, is God calling you to maintain an attitude of thanksgiving?

Day 4: Thankful That God is with Me in the Storms

What are three things you are thankful for today?

You're either coming out of a storm, in the middle of one, or there's a storm on the horizon. Life's journey can be challenging, bringing "storms" of all kinds—divorce, depression, financial struggles, family conflicts, health battles, anxiety, and more. Often, we may find ourselves wanting the storm to simply pass. During these times, it's easy to question where God is or even blame Him for the storm.

Never allow the presence of a storm to make you doubt the presence of God.

Read: Acts 27:13-26
In this passage, Paul and a crew of men find themselves in a massive storm while on a boat—a storm they thought they would not survive.

"When neither sun nor stars appeared for many days and the storm continued raging..."

Have you ever faced a storm that seemed endless? What situations or challenges come to mind?

_____

"But now I urge you to keep up your courage."
Could you use this encouragement today? Keep up your courage; this storm will not take you down.

Paul tells the crew that an angel of the Lord appeared to assure him that God still had plans for him; therefore, this storm would not be his end.
If God gave you breath today, He's not done with you. He has plans for you, and no storm can derail His purposes. You will not be overcome by this trial. God has more for you—more people to serve, more lives to impact. Your ship may struggle in the storm, but this storm will not destroy you. In fact, God may use it to prepare you to help others in their own storms. He is strengthening your faith and equipping you to be a blessing to others.

"Praise be to the God and Father of our Lord Jesus Christ, the Father of compassion and the God of all comfort, who comforts us in all our troubles, so that we can comfort those in any trouble with the comfort we ourselves receive from God."
—2 Corinthians 1:3-4

Keep up your courage and be thankful for a God who not only stands with you through life's storms but also uses them to strengthen and bless you. God's presence can be seen in so many ways: through His Spirit, in answered prayers, as He goes before you, and as He guides your steps.

In another story about a different storm, we find Jesus asleep in the boat's stern.

Read: Mark 4:35-41

In this passage, the disciples panic as the storm rages.
"Don't you care, Jesus? Aren't you going to do anything about this storm?"
These are familiar questions that we, too, may ask during life's storms.

With just a few words—*"Peace! Be still!"*—Jesus brought calm to the storm.
Is there a situation in which He may currently be speaking these words to you? "Peace. Be still."

Peace isn't found in the absence of a storm; it's found in the presence of Jesus. Real peace does not come from a trouble-free life. Following Jesus doesn't mean we'll never experience bad days. Instead, real peace is found in knowing that Jesus is with us, right beside us, never leaving or forsaking us.

Our faith is not in the stability of our "boat;" it's in the One who commands the wind and the waves. Praise God for seeing us through every trial, for providing in our need, for bringing healing, and for being our peace in the midst of the storm.

Take a few moments now to sit in quiet reflection, asking the Lord to fill you with His profound peace, no matter the storm.

Day 5: Grateful That I Don't Need to Be Perfect

What are three things you are grateful for today?

Do you find yourself battling an unhealthy need to live up to expectations? Expectations from others, from God, or even the standards you set for yourself? Are you hard on yourself when you mess up or don't do things perfectly? Perhaps you show grace to others, yet struggle to extend that same grace to yourself, carrying guilt, shame, or a sense of unworthiness when you fall short.

Many of us feel intense pressure: to maintain a picture-perfect home, appearance, career, family, exercise routine, or social life. And often, it leads to one of three responses:

1. **Sustaining a False Image** – Always striving to keep up appearances or maintain a certain image, often one that isn't fully true.
2. **Avoiding Risks or Challenges** – Not attempting something meaningful out of fear it won't meet high standards.

3. **Obsessing Over Details** – Fixating on getting things "just right," sometimes to the point of ineffectiveness.

Which of these responses do you find yourself relating to most often? Do any of these tendencies show up in your life?

In addition to our responses, perfectionists tend to fall into three categories:

- **Self-Oriented Perfectionists:** Those who place high expectations on themselves, often struggling with feelings of inadequacy and guilt.
- **Externally-Oriented Perfectionists:** Those who feel others expect them to be perfect. They may feel overwhelmed, isolated, or believe they will never meet others' expectations.
- **Others-Oriented Perfectionists:** Those who impose their high expectations on others, often lacking empathy and struggling with frustration when others don't meet their standards.

Which category resonates with you, and how does it affect your daily life?

At its core, perfectionism can be a spiritual problem, often a covering for deep fears or insecurities. It can mask our insecurities, becoming a way to feel "good enough." But God doesn't call us to live with this weight. Instead, He offers us **grace**. Perfectionism centers on our efforts, our achievements, and our abilities, while grace shifts the focus to what Jesus has already done. Grace frees us to live from a place of acceptance, secure in the knowledge that we are loved and approved by God.

In the story of Martha and Mary, Jesus reminded Martha of this very truth:

Read: Luke 10:38-42

"My dear Martha, you are worried and upset over all these details! There is only one thing worth being concerned about. Mary has discovered it, and it will not be taken away from her."

Jesus wants us to choose people over perfection, relationships over image. He doesn't want us to miss moments of true connection because we're focused on achieving or appearing "perfect."

The holiday season can intensify this struggle. But what if we chose to let go? What if we stopped worrying about appearances, prioritizing relationships instead? Our goal isn't perfect performance; it's perfect love.

Read: Matthew 5:43-48

"You have heard that it was said, 'Love your neighbor and hate your enemy.' But I tell you, love your enemies and pray for those who persecute you… Be perfect, therefore, as your heavenly Father is perfect."

In this context, "perfect" doesn't mean flawless performance; it's about the completeness of our love. Jesus calls us to be whole in our love for others, to love freely and generously, as we have been loved.

God invites us to turn our gaze from ourselves and focus on Jesus. In Him, you are free—free to live and serve imperfectly.

Where in your life is God calling you to let go of perfection, to release the need to meet certain standards or seek approval? What would it look like to lay that down at His feet today?

You will never be enough, and you don't need to be. Your calling is not to be perfect. Your calling is not to convince others of how good you are; your calling is to convince others of how good God is. Spend some time with the Lord right now. What burden is He calling you to lay at His feet this holiday season.

The Heart of Christmas

4 Weeks of Joy and Meaning

Week 1:
Hope

Day 1: Hope for a Messiah

The holiday season often becomes a whirlwind of activity—shopping, wrapping gifts, baking cookies, and decorating. We fill our homes with lights and send out cards, all while juggling the festive chaos. But in the midst of all this, how are we preparing spiritually? We know it's important to remember "the reason for the season," yet we often find ourselves feeling drained, our souls weary and disconnected from the One we are supposed to be celebrating.

Does this resonate with you? How do you usually feel during the holiday season? What would you like to experience this Christmas?

Read: Genesis 3

This is probably a familiar passage to you. You might feel the temptation to skim it, thinking you already know the story. But today, read it with fresh eyes. Ask God to show you something new. Take a moment and write down at least one insight that stands out to you.

Ever since the events in Genesis 3, our world has been weary. Adam and Eve's disobedience shattered their intimate connection with God. They no longer lived in perfect harmony with Him or His creation. And because of sin, every person is born separated from God.

"Then the Lord God said to the serpent,
'Because you have done this,
you are cursed more than all animals,
domestic and wild.
You will crawl on your belly,
groveling in the dust as long as you live.
And I will cause hostility between you and the woman,
and between your offspring and her offspring.
He will strike your head,
and you will strike his heel.'"
—*Genesis 3:14-15*

Take a moment to reflect. How do you understand these verses? What do you think verse 15 means?

In response to the serpent's deception, God pronounced a curse on the serpent—and on Satan, who took the serpent's form. God foretold that there would be ongoing enmity between the offspring of the woman and the serpent. And in verse 15, we read a powerful prophecy:

"He will crush your head, and you will strike his heel."

This verse is a hint of what is to come—a promise that Satan would harm humanity's savior, but ultimately, the savior would defeat Satan.

When Eve gave birth to her first son, Cain, she said, *"With the Lord's help, I have brought forth a man."* (Genesis 4:1). Some commentators believe that Eve may have thought Cain was the promised deliverer—the one who would crush the serpent's head. But Cain, instead of being the savior, became the first murderer. The long wait for the Messiah had only just begun.

This wait is the foundation of our hope. Since Genesis 3, God's people have longed for the promised Messiah. And in the Christmas season, we remember that hope—the hope of Christ's first coming.

Can you recall a time in your life when you were in a season of waiting? Perhaps a time of hope deferred? Reflect on the emotions you experienced during that time. What did God teach you?

"He will crush your head,
and you will strike his heel."

God's final curse to the serpent foretold the coming of Christ. While Satan would strike at Jesus (symbolizing Christ's suffering and death), Jesus would ultimately triumph, defeating Satan through His death and resurrection.

As we enter this season of Advent, let us take time to reflect on the long years of waiting that God's people endured. Let that deepen our gratitude for Jesus' coming. But also remember, we are in our own season of waiting—for Christ's return, when He will establish His kingdom on earth.

"We know that the whole creation has been groaning as in the pains of childbirth right up to the present time. Not only so, but we ourselves, who have the firstfruits of the Spirit, groan inwardly as we wait eagerly for our adoption to sonship, the redemption of our bodies. For in this hope we were saved. But hope that is seen is no hope at all. Who hopes for what they already have? But if we hope for what we do not yet have, we wait for it patiently."
—*Romans 8:22-25*

Take some time now to sit quietly at Jesus' feet. Ask Him to reveal to you the true hope that He offers. Close your time in prayer, reflecting on what He may be saying to your heart today.

Day 2: Hope in Silence

Have you ever found yourself waiting a long time in prayer? What were you praying for? How did you feel during that time—forgotten, discouraged, maybe even hopeless or angry?

Read: Psalm 13

Have you ever felt similar to the emotions expressed in this Psalm?

Notice how David shifts his focus in the final verses. Where does he ultimately place his hope?

God's people have often experienced long seasons of waiting and silence from Him. One of the most significant periods of silence was the 400 years between the books of Malachi and Matthew. During this time, no prophets spoke, and it might have seemed as though God had forgotten His people. However, a lot was happening that would set the stage for the New Testament. Judea was ruled by various foreign powers, from the Persians to the Romans, and the Old Testament was translated into Greek, known as the Septuagint, the version most often quoted in the New Testament. Though it may have seemed like God was absent, He wasn't. He remembered His people and the promises He had made.

Read: Malachi 4:5-6

"See, I will send you the prophet Elijah before that great and dreadful day of the Lord comes."
—Malachi 4:5

In the chapters leading up to this, Malachi condemns the spiritual apathy of Israel. The priests had become corrupt, the people were breaking their marriage covenants, oppressing others, and neglecting their tithes. But God, through Malachi, promises hope to those who remain faithful. He foretells the coming of Elijah, the great prophet who would prepare the way for the Lord.

"And he will go on before the Lord, in the spirit and power of Elijah, to turn the hearts of the parents to their children and the disobedient to the wisdom of the righteous—to make ready a people prepared for the Lord."
—Luke 1:17

Jesus later confirms that Elijah had come, referring to John the Baptist:

"But I tell you, Elijah has already come, and they did not recognize him... In the same way, the Son of Man is going to suffer at their hands."
—Matthew 17:12-13

For 400 years, God's faithful had to wait. It was a time of patience and expectation, but hope remained.

Read: Micah 5:2-4

"But you, O Bethlehem Ephrathah,
are only a small village among all the people of Judah.
Yet a ruler of Israel,
whose origins are in the distant past,
will come from you on my behalf.
The people of Israel will be abandoned to their enemies
until the woman in labor gives birth.
Then at last his fellow countrymen
will return from exile to their own land.
And he will stand to lead his flock with the Lord's strength,
in the majesty of the name of the Lord his God.
Then his people will live there undisturbed,
for he will be highly honored around the world."

Matthew also references this passage when he recounts the birth of Jesus:

"Jesus was born in Bethlehem in Judea, during the reign of King Herod...
'Where is the Messiah supposed to be born?'
'In Bethlehem in Judea,' they said, 'for this is what the prophet wrote...'"
—Matthew 2:1-6

These passages come together to show us that God keeps His promises, even when it feels like He's silent. The prophecy of the Messiah's birth, first given in Micah, was fulfilled in Matthew. We can trust that God's yet-unfulfilled promises will also come to pass.

As you reflect on the 400 years of silence between the Old and New Testaments, consider your own seasons of waiting. Has there been a time in your life when God seemed silent?

Looking back, can you now see how He was working, even when it wasn't clear at the time?

How might your past experiences of waiting help you navigate current situations where you feel like you are still waiting for God to respond?

Day 3: Hope in God's Plan

Read: Isaiah 53

Isaiah wrote this chapter around 700 years before the birth of Christ. It's often referred to as the "5th Gospel" because of its clear prophetic connection to Jesus.

In verse 2, the Messiah is described: "He had no form or majesty that we should look at Him, and no beauty that we should desire Him." Why do you think this description is significant?

What does Scripture say about why Jesus came to earth? Let's explore a few key passages:

Matthew 26:28
"For this is My blood, which confirms the covenant between God and His people. It is poured out as a sacrifice to forgive the sins of many."

John 1:29
"Look! The Lamb of God who takes away the sin of the world!"

John 10:10
"The thief comes only to steal and kill and destroy; I have come that they may have life, and have it to the full."

———————————

Take another look at Isaiah 53 and note the many ways the "suffering servant" endured hardship.

Now, read **Matthew 27:26-35**. What parallels can you see between the suffering described in Isaiah 53 and the suffering Jesus experienced during His crucifixion?

There is a great plan and purpose behind Jesus' birth, ministry, and death. His death was not a tragic event without meaning—it was a necessity, a divine plan for our redemption.

As you conclude today's reflection, reread **Isaiah 53:5-6** and **10-12**. Afterward, take a few moments to sit quietly, reflecting on all that Jesus is and the hope He brings.

Isaiah 53:5-6
"But He was pierced for our rebellion,
crushed for our sins.
He was beaten so we could be whole.
He was whipped so we could be healed.
All of us, like sheep, have strayed away.
We have left God's paths to follow our own.
Yet the Lord laid on Him the sins of us all."

Isaiah 53:10-12

"But it was the Lord's good plan to crush Him
and cause Him grief.
Yet when His life is made an offering for sin,
He will have many descendants.
He will enjoy a long life,
and the Lord's good plan will prosper in His hands.
When He sees all that is accomplished by His anguish,
He will be satisfied.
And because of His experience,
My righteous servant will make it possible
for many to be counted righteous,
for He will bear all their sins.
I will give Him the honors of a victorious soldier,
because He exposed Himself to death.
He was counted among the rebels.
He bore the sins of many
and interceded for rebels."

Day 4: Hope While Waiting

Read: Deuteronomy 31:1-8

Moses gave Joshua a promise in this passage, and this promise remained true even during the 400 years between the Old Testament and the Gospel of Matthew, known as the Intertestamental Period. Although it seemed like God was absent, He wasn't. He hadn't forgotten His promise. God was preparing to send a rescuer, a second Elijah, to deliver His people. This began a long period of waiting and hope for God's people.

Read: Galatians 4:4-6

"But when the time came to completion, God sent his Son, born of a woman, born under the law, to redeem those under the law, so that we might receive adoption as sons. And because you are sons, God sent the Spirit of his Son into our hearts, crying, 'Abba, Father!'"
—*Galatians 4:4-6*

What do you think the phrase *"when the time came to completion"* means? Why do you think Jesus was born when He was?

God may have seemed silent during the Intertestamental Period, and He may seem silent at times in our own lives. But during those 400 years, a great deal was happening. The Persians conquered the Babylonians, and then the Greeks conquered the Persians. Cultural and ideological changes occurred, and religious views shifted. The Scriptures were translated into other languages. When the Romans took rule around 63 BC, hope was low for God's people, and they desperately awaited the coming Messiah. But God had been preparing His people. After years of silence, the Word was about to come alive.

Reflect on your past. How has God used periods of waiting, silence, or change in your life to prepare you?

God is always doing 10,000 things in your life, and you may only be aware of three of them. How might God be preparing you right now for what He wants in your future?

"Before I formed you in the womb I knew you,
before you were born I set you apart."
—Jeremiah 1:5

"For I know the plans I have for you," declares the Lord, "plans to prosper you and not to harm you, plans to give you hope and a future."
—Jeremiah 29:11

"And we know that in all things God works for the good of those who love him, who have been called according to his purpose."
—*Romans 8:28*

"Trust in the Lord with all your heart
and lean not on your own understanding;
in all your ways submit to him,
and he will make your paths straight."
—*Proverbs 3:5-6*

God had a plan then, and God has a plan now—for you and for all He wants to accomplish in your life. Your hope in the Lord stands on a solid foundation!

Close your time in prayer. Where is God calling you to develop a greater hope while waiting for changes in your life?

Day 5: Hope in Darkness

Read: Isaiah 9:1-7

*"The people walking in darkness have seen a great light;
a light has dawned on those living in the land of darkness."*
—*Isaiah 9:2*

Isaiah's prophecies brought messages of hope—a hope of a coming light in the midst of darkness, a light that dispels the fear and anxiety darkness can bring.

Read: John 8:12

"When Jesus spoke again to the people, he said, 'I am the light of the world. Whoever follows me will never walk in darkness, but will have the light of life.'"
—*John 8:12*

Go through Isaiah 9:1-5 and circle all the words that describe darkness or pain.

Each verse in this passage speaks about a promise. Verse 9:1 spoke about honor; 9:2 about light. What promise is revealed in 9:3?

_____

Isaiah refers to the battle with Midian in this passage.

Read: Judges 7.
What made this battle so unique?

Isaiah also prophesied other names for the light mentioned in verse 2. Reflect on the names of Jesus listed in Isaiah 9:6. Consider each name and how Jesus fulfilled that role during His ministry on earth. Have you personally experienced any of these descriptions of Jesus in your life?

Wonderful Counselor

Mighty God

Eternal Father

Prince of Peace

Reflect on the following lyrics from the song *"Reckless Love."*
Do you feel the Lord's zeal in these words?

————————————

From here to there
Worship is filling the atmosphere
Both now and then
Songs of your love will never end
All day and night
As we bow down our praise will rise
Inside and out
All that I am will shout

Let my worship rise
Like a sweet perfume
I'll pour my love
My love
All over you

OH he chases me down fights till I'm found
Leaves the ninety-nine
I couldn't earn it
I don't deserve it
Still you gave yourself away
Oh the overwhelming
Never-ending
Reckless love of God

Oh good God you're amazing God...
No shadow you won't light up
Mountain you won't climb up
Coming after me

No wall you won't kick down
Lie you won't tear down
Coming after me

There is nothing our Mighty God and Loving Father wouldn't do to draw you to Him. What incredible hope we have in the Lord Jesus!

Spend a few moments quietly with the Lord. Can you feel His presence today?

Week 2: Peace and Preparation

Day 1: Preparing Our Hearts for God

Read: Isaiah 40:1-5 & Luke 2:1-7

Just like Mary and Joseph awaiting the birth of Jesus, as we await the celebration of His birth, we must also prepare. Just as one wouldn't plant a seed and expect a harvest the next morning, we need to prepare our hearts to receive the Lord. Luke's account of the birth of Jesus tells us why He was born in a stable—there was no room for them at the inn. As you move through this wonderful, yet busy, season, is there room for Jesus in your heart? It is no less ironic that Jesus can be on the periphery of our holiday schedules than it was that He, the Son of David, lay in a manger on the periphery of the city of David.

As you prepare for Christmas and all that God has in store for you in the new year, focus on preparing your heart. Here are a few ways to do that:

Diminish distractions.
The stress of the Christmas season can easily distract you from what's really important. Spend a few extra minutes in your morning quiet time with the Lord. Spend more time with family. Simplify as much as possible. Notice when the holiday becomes too commercial. Be still and listen for God's voice. Keep your "eyes on Jesus, the source and perfecter of faith."

42

"Therefore, since we are surrounded by such a great cloud of witnesses, let us throw off everything that hinders and the sin that so easily entangles. And let us run with perseverance the race marked out for us, fixing our eyes on Jesus, the pioneer and perfecter of faith."
—Hebrews 12:1-2

What are a few realistic and tangible steps you can take to diminish distractions and focus on the true beauty and meaning of this season? Is there something you could eliminate to free up time in your schedule or your heart?

Reflect on God's presence.
Look back on this past year. Perhaps you've faced financial difficulty, illness, or a time of suffering. How has God carried you through? Can you look back and see His presence? Remember Joseph's words in Genesis: *"You planned evil against me; God planned it for good..."* (Genesis 50:20). Where do you see God's hand at work in your life this past year?

Seek God first, then slow down.
Do you approach the holiday season more like Martha—frazzled and busy—or more like Mary—seeking the presence of the Lord?

"As Jesus and his disciples were on their way, he came to a village where a woman named Martha opened her home to him. She had a sister called Mary, who sat at the Lord's feet listening to what he said. But Martha was distracted by all the preparations that had to be made. She came to him and asked, 'Lord, don't you care that my sister has left me to do the work by myself? Tell her to help me!'

'Martha, Martha,' the Lord answered, 'you are worried and upset about many things, but few things are needed—or indeed only one. Mary has chosen what is better, and it will not be taken away from her.'"
—*Luke 10:38-42*

In what situations during the holiday season do you find yourself acting more like Martha? Where is Jesus in those moments for you? Where is His peace? Is His love flowing through you to others? Can you think of ways to act more like Mary in these situations?

Consider those in need.
"In everything I did, I showed you that by this kind of hard work we must help the weak, remembering the words the Lord Jesus himself said: 'It is more blessed to give than to receive.'"
—*Acts 20:35*

"For I was hungry and you gave me something to eat, I was thirsty and you gave me something to drink, I was a stranger and you invited me in, I needed clothes and you clothed me, I was sick and you looked after me, I was in prison and you came to visit me.
The King will reply, 'Truly I tell you, whatever you did for one of the least of these brothers and sisters of mine, you did for me.'"
—*Matthew 25:35-40*

How can you serve the Lord by serving others during this season? Is there a charity you can donate your time or resources to? Is there someone who might need a helping hand or companionship? Could you and your family or friends make a positive impact on the life of someone less fortunate?

Read: Revelation 3:20

"Here I am! I stand at the door and knock. If anyone hears my voice and opens the door, I will come in and eat with that person, and they with me."
—*Revelation 3:20*

The Lord is waiting at the door. Can you be still enough to hear His voice? You may need to say "no" to certain things on your to-do list to say "yes" to the gift God is offering. This season is a unique opportunity to reflect on the birth of Christ and the gift He brings. While we can reflect on the Savior's birth any day of the year, do we? Can you slow down enough during this season to open the door and allow the Lord to take center stage, giving Him your attention, gratitude, and joy? Chances are, this season will feel more blessed, peaceful, joyful, and meaningful if you do.

Day 2: Peace in Difficult Situations

Read: Luke 2:8-21

"Silent night, holy night
All is calm, all is bright
'Round yon virgin Mother and Child
Holy infant so tender and mild
Sleep in heavenly peace"

Sometimes the busyness of the season can leave us feeling anything but peaceful. It's common to feel busy, rushed, frazzled, and worn out. And it's not just during this most wonderful time of the year— many people feel like they're simply "getting by" in their day-to-day lives, hurriedly moving from one task to another. It can feel like you're holding your breath, just trying to make it through a difficult situation before you can exhale.

Have you ever found yourself holding your breath or pushing through tough times without a sense of peace? When?
How would your trying situations or day-to-day living look different if you were filled with a sense of peace rather than tension or weariness? How would your experience change? How would others see you differently?

_____

Throughout Scripture, God promises us His peace. Reread Luke 2:13-14.

"...and on earth _____ to those on whom his favor rests."

God's favor rests on you! The heavenly praises come right after the angel of the Lord delivers the news of Christ's birth. Peace was a big part of Christ's coming. The Prince of Peace came to bring us peace.

When we doubt God's promise of peace—or just don't sense it—it's often because we're trying to handle life's situations in our own strength. The peace we seek is often a solution to our problems, rather than a quiet heart in the midst of them. But God's peace comes from Jesus' victory over sin, evil, and death. His victory is bigger than any problem we face. We can take a deep breath and rest in God's strength and victory.

"I have told you these things, so that in me you may have peace. In this world you will have trouble. But take heart! I have overcome the world."
—John 16:33

How can this verse bring you peace in your current situations and circumstances?

Read: Matthew 14:27-31
Can you see the connection between faith, hope, and peace? In what ways does a lack of faith hold you back from living with a heart characterized by hope and grounded in peace?

"You will keep in perfect peace
those whose minds are steadfast,
because they trust in you."
—Isaiah 26:3

"Do not be anxious about anything, but in every situation, by prayer and
petition, with thanksgiving, present your requests to God. And the peace of
God, which transcends all understanding, will guard your hearts and your
minds in Christ Jesus."
—Philippians 4:6-7

How does prayer bring you peace?

There is nothing too big or too small to bring to God in prayer. He can handle your burdens and frustrations. He wants to walk with you through your difficult circumstances and help you experience His peace. This season is the perfect time to bring your worries to the Lord. Lay your heart open before Him. Ask Him to help you trust Him more fully and experience His true peace, which transcends our limited understanding.

Day 3: Celebrate Your Peace with God

"For to us a child is born,
to us a son is given,
and the government will be on his shoulders.
And he will be called
Wonderful Counselor, Mighty God,
Everlasting Father, Prince of Peace."
—Isaiah 9:6

Why do you think Jesus is described as the Prince of Peace? How do you personally experience Him as the Prince of Peace?

Read: Matthew 10:34-39

What a surprising statement! Jesus said, *"I did not come to bring peace, but a sword!"* Why would He say that? What do you make of this verse?

"Therefore, since we have been justified through faith, we have peace with God through our Lord Jesus Christ."
—Romans 5:1

When Jesus said that He did not come to bring peace, but a sword, He was addressing false assumptions about the Messiah's mission. The Jewish people often interpreted passages like Isaiah 9:5-7 to mean the Messiah would bring political and social peace on earth. However, that wasn't Jesus' mission. The ultimate goal of the Gospel was—and is—peace with God, not earthly harmony.

Peace is often thought of as stillness or quiet, defined by an absence of disturbance or chaos. In the beginning, there was peace. Before Genesis 3, there was peace on Earth and peace between humanity and God. This peace wasn't merely stillness; it was nearness to God. God walked with Adam and Eve in the cool of the day. They enjoyed unrestricted access to Him. This peace with God was disrupted by their sin, and now we are in the same situation as Adam and Eve after the fall—separated from God by sin and lacking peace with Him.

Read: Romans 3:21-28

God's holiness demands perfection, which is why sin separates us from Him.

Read: Ephesians 2:11-22

What is the difference between having peace with God and feeling peaceful? Are they always present together?

If you are a follower of Christ, you have peace with God. This peace isn't temporary or fleeting; it is unchanging and unwavering. God is worthy to be praised for His gift of peace and redemption through Christ. Can you celebrate that gift today? Consider spending extra time in prayer, thanking Him, talking about your joy with your family over dinner, or sharing a moment of gratitude with friends. You have peace with God—celebrate this truth today!

Day 4: Peace in God Immanuel

Read: Luke 1:5-25

Generation after generation, God's people waited to be rescued, hoping for the promised Messiah. As far back as Genesis 3:15, God told Satan, *"I will put enmity between you and the woman, and between your offspring and hers; he will crush your head, and you will strike his heel."* In other words: a child of Eve (Jesus) will one day defeat you, Satan, and I will rescue my people.

God's people needed and longed to be rescued. They believed God would send a Messiah to restore peace, but they sometimes forgot and needed reminders. God sent prophets and judges to renew His promises. Then, after a long period of silence, God broke His silence through the angel Gabriel, who appeared to Zechariah.

What are the first things the angel Gabriel said to Zechariah?

We can only wonder what Zechariah's prayers entailed. Had he been praying all this time for a son? For the salvation of God's people? For the coming Messiah? Whatever his prayers were, in one statement from Gabriel, they were about to be answered. But before telling Zechariah that his prayer has been heard, Gabriel says, *"Do not be afraid."*

God was paving the way for all people to have peace with Him. Zechariah's son, John, would prepare the way for the Rescuer, the Messiah whom God's people had long been awaiting.

Read: Luke 1:26-38

Now Gabriel appears to Mary, the mother of Jesus. Mary was understandably frightened and troubled by Gabriel's sudden greeting. But what does he tell her in verse 30?

Gabriel doesn't just tell Mary not to be afraid. How does he further reassure her? Copy verse 37 below:

Read: Matthew 1:18-25
What does the angel tell Joseph in verse 20? What does the word Immanuel mean (verse 23)?

All these angelic messages urge us not to fear. The Rescuer, the One who saves us from our sins, the Messiah, our Immanuel, is now with us. Peace has arrived, and we now have peace with God. Glory be to God—what a gift we have in Christ!

To conclude today, spend a few moments reflecting on the lyrics of the song *"Breath of Heaven"* by Amy Grant. Imagine Mary, young and perhaps scared, praying these words to God.

I have traveled many moonless nights
Cold and weary with a babe inside
And I wonder what I've done
Holy Father, you have come
And chosen me now to carry your son

I am waiting in a silent prayer
I am frightened by the load I bear
In a world as cold as stone
Must I walk this path alone?
Be with me now
Breath of heaven
Hold me together
Be forever near me
Breath of heaven

Breath of heaven
Lighten my darkness
Pour over me your holiness
For you are holy
Breath of heaven

Do you wonder as you watch my face
If a wiser one should have had my place
But I offer all I am
For the mercy of your plan
Help me be strong
Help me be
Help me

Breath of heaven
Hold me together
Be forever near...

Which portions—lines or phrases—could you lift up to God yourself?

Day 5: Perfect Peace

"In the beginning God created the heavens and the earth."
—*Genesis 1:1*

Read: Matthew 1:18-23 & John 1:1-14

In John 1, John refers to Jesus as "The Word" (logos in Greek) three times. This term, *logos*, held profound meaning for the Jews. To them, *logos* represented the word by which God:

- spoke the world into existence,
- guided the prophets,
- and delivered His people.

Using *logos* would certainly catch their attention. The phrase "the word of God" was often used to refer to God Himself. So, to say *"The Word became flesh and made his dwelling among us"* was the same as saying, *"God became flesh and made His dwelling among us."*

Notice how John 1:1-2 highlights Jesus' deity: *"In the beginning was the Word, and the Word was with God, and the Word was God."* This passage establishes that Jesus, while distinct from the Father, is also fully God. These verses form one of the most foundational truths of our faith—the Trinity. While each has differing roles, the Father and the Son are equally God, yet distinct persons. Jesus existed from the beginning, He was with God, and He was God.

55

While verses 1-2 emphasize Jesus' deity—*"the Word was God"*—verse 14 emphasizes Jesus' humanity—*"The Word became flesh."* Jesus didn't just appear as a man; He was fully human, 100% God and 100% man. This profound truth is at the core of Christianity.

_____

"For since death came through a man, the resurrection of the dead comes also through a man. For as in Adam all die, so in Christ all will be made alive."
—*1 Corinthians 15:21-22*

Since death came through a man, the resurrection of the dead also had to come through a _____.

Sin came into the world through a man, Adam, and as his descendants, we all inherit a sinful nature. Just as sin entered through man, it had to be removed by a man. If Christ had come as a purely spiritual being, He could not have been sacrificed for our sins. If He weren't truly human, He would not have had blood to shed.

"In fact, the law requires that nearly everything be cleansed with blood, and without the shedding of blood there is no forgiveness."
—*Hebrews 9:22*

During His ministry, Jesus' humanity was evident to those who saw, heard, touched, and shared life with Him. But what wasn't immediately apparent was that He was also fully God. After His ascension, however, questions arose about His humanity, and early Christians, who began by accepting His deity, sometimes struggled with the fullness of His humanness.

Do you tend to struggle with one of these views of Jesus more than the other—that He is fully human but also fully God?

Have we today lost some of our wonder at the true humanity of Christ, Immanuel, God with us? This Christmas season is a perfect time to stand in awe and wonder as we contemplate our Savior, God who took on human flesh to save us from our sins. He became fully man to save us fully.

In John's Gospel, Jesus was preparing His disciples for His death and return to the Father. Just as one might hope to prepare loved ones for their passing by sharing important words, Jesus was ensuring His disciples knew what mattered most. He spoke to them of a new commandment, of the way to the Father, and the coming of the Holy Spirit. He wanted them to understand who He was and how to carry on after His death.

Read: John 14:1-27

What was Jesus' promised gift to His disciples in verse 27? He offers you this same gift now. He offers you His peace and tells you not to be afraid, not to be worried, not to be anxious.

What fears, worries, or anxieties could you lift before the Lord today? Close your time in prayer, asking Jesus to help you sense His peace and to lessen your anxiety.

Week 3: Joy

Day 1: Be Joyful

Read: Acts 13:14-33

In these verses, Paul speaks boldly and passionately about God. With confidence, he proclaims, *"We tell you the good news: What God promised our ancestors he has fulfilled for us, their children, by raising up Jesus."* Paul uses the history of what God has done to share the good news of Jesus.

How can knowing the Bible give you confidence and joy? Can you think of a time when you experienced a sense of joy because of your knowledge of Scripture or because of the ways in which you have personally experienced God working in your life?

Read: Acts 13:42-52

Paul and Barnabas boldly shared the gospel despite opposition, trusting that God could use them to spread His word. In what ways do you feel God might be calling you to share His message with others? Consider the unique opportunities in your life—your relationships, workplace, or community—where you might be able to reflect His truth and love.

How do you feel God could use you to share His message with those around you?

———————————

Why did Paul and Barnabas leave the city full of joy, even though they were kicked out?

Paul and Barnabas experienced joy even in the face of rejection, knowing they were fulfilling God's call to share His message. Joy can flow not only from sharing the gospel but also from acts of kindness, encouragement, and love. How might God be calling you to bring joy to others, whether through sharing His word or through your actions? Consider specific situations where He could use you to be a source of joy—think of 3-5 ways you could bring His light to those around you.

We are called to be joyful. We are called to be peacemakers and to bring joy and peace to others. But being joyful doesn't mean living a life free of problems, disappointments, or hardships. Trials and difficulties are not intended as punishments. In fact, Scripture is clear that even the obedient will suffer. We will face trials, troubles, and challenges.

Read: 1 Peter 2:18-25

According to this passage, what brings favor from God? (v20)

_____

Can you remember a time when your obedience brought hurt or suffering? How did you react?

Read: 2 Corinthians 4:8-12

What in your life has you feeling hard-pressed or weighed down?

Remember: You are not crushed; God's strength lives in you.

What in your life is leaving you feeling perplexed, uncertain, or perhaps confused about where God is in this particular situation?

Remember: God sees what you cannot see. God knows what you do not know. He is in control and has a plan for you.

When have you felt abandoned, alone, or knocked down by others or by life's circumstances?

—————————————

—————————————

Remember: God will never leave you nor forsake you. When you look back and see only one set of footprints in the sand, they were His footprints as He lovingly carried you.

Rejoice and be glad, for He who began a good work in you will be faithful to complete it. God will use you—and your joyfulness—to be a blessing in the lives of others. His strength and presence will keep you from ever needing to rely solely on your own strength.

Close your time in prayer, asking God where or with whom He is calling you to be more joyful.

Day 2: Good News of Great Joy

"Don't be afraid, for look, I proclaim to you good news of great joy that will be for all the people."
—*Luke 2:10*

Jesus was born among us, lived a perfect life, and was crucified for our sins. He taught, healed, and performed miracles. He died on the cross as a sacrifice for our sins, and three days later rose again, proving He is Lord over even death.

"I passed on to you what was most important and what had also been passed on to me. Christ died for our sins, just as the Scriptures said. He was buried, and he was raised from the dead on the third day, just as the Scriptures said."
—*1 Corinthians 15:3-4*

All of this happened *"according to the Scriptures,"* and this is truly news of great joy and celebration! As we celebrate the coming of the Son of God to earth this week, let us join the angels and the shepherds in praising and worshiping God for the great joy that has come to us.

We often equate joy with happy or positive circumstances. We might recall some of our most joyful memories as times like getting married, the birth of a child, or a special family trip.

But is it possible to have joy even in the midst of pain? In God's kingdom, joy comes from following Him and serving others.

Can you think of a time when you experienced joy in the midst of pain, suffering, or a difficult situation, or a time when serving others brought you joy? How would you describe that joy?

Read: Psalm 23

Consider how the Lord has been your shepherd.

Can you recall a specific time when the Lord protected you, either physically or emotionally? How did you recognize His protection in that situation?

Think of a particular moment when you felt guided by God's wisdom or direction. How did He lead you, and what difference did it make?

Reflect on a season of challenge or uncertainty—can you identify a way that the Lord provided comfort or reassurance during that time? How did His presence bring peace or strength?

Regardless of your circumstances, troubles, or unmet expectations, the Lord is your Shepherd and seeks to bring you joy and peace.

Read: Psalm 96
How can we find joy in worship, as stated in this Psalm?

"Rejoice in the Lord always: and again I say, Rejoice!"
—Philippians 4:4

As you prepare your heart for Christmas morning, can you commit to having a heart of joy? Can you commit to being a "joy-giver," sharing your deep inner joy with others? What changes do you need to make to live with more joy?

Day 3: Joy in Service

Read: John 13:1-17

Who do you think usually washed feet in the first century? Did Jesus have to wash feet? Why did He do it? What does this tell you about the nature and attitude of Jesus?

Why didn't any of the disciples think to offer to wash feet? What were some of the other disciples doing during this meal?

"Then they began to argue among themselves about who would be the greatest among them."
—Luke 22:24

How does this behavior resonate with you, or how might it sometimes show up in your life, preventing you from humbly serving others and putting their needs above your own?

What was Peter's reaction when Jesus came to wash his feet? Why did Peter react the way he did? How would you respond?

"Now that I, your Lord and Teacher, have washed your feet, you also should wash one another's feet. I have set you an example that you should do as I have done for you."

Jesus isn't commanding that we literally wash feet. What is He teaching His disciples (and all of us) to do?

What would be an example of something equivalent to washing feet in the first century that most people would not be willing to do today? And what are everyday examples in your own life that might be equivalent to washing feet? Have you ever found yourself unwilling to do something that Jesus would have done if He were in your shoes?

How does seeing Jesus serve and love His disciples help you understand how you are called to serve and love people in your life? Spend a moment in prayer. Who is God calling you to love more humbly right now?

Read: Philippians 2:3-11
How is this passage similar to John 13:1-17?

In our opening passage (John 13:1-17), Jesus knew His hour had come. He demonstrated great love to His disciples through service, giving them a deeper understanding of what it means to serve, to love, and to be blessed.

Consider:
If you knew you had less than 24 hours left to live, would you choose to serve others? That's what Jesus did.

If you knew you had all authority from God, would you humble yourself as a servant and serve those around you? That's what Jesus did.

Would you serve someone knowing they would betray you? That's what Jesus did.

If we are seeking true joy, it won't be found in self-service and gratification. Serving others may not seem fulfilling at first, but when we adopt the mindset of Christ, honoring others above ourselves, we find peace and joy in serving. Jesus promises this joy: *"If you know these things, you are blessed if you do them."* Blessed, happy, joyful.

May this be a season filled with blessing, happiness, and joy!

Day 4: Joy is Contagious

Read: Psalm 126

God works in our lives in countless ways. He answers prayers, comforts us with His presence, and offers healing. He brings the right person or experience into our lives at just the right time. He provides a way out or an open door. There are so many ways He makes His power known, and when He does, we can't help but be filled with the joy that comes from knowing He is who He says He is, that He is with us, and that He loves us.

What are some examples of ways God has worked in your life?

Has He answered prayers, provided healing, an open door, or just the right comfort or support at the right time? List a few examples here:

When the psalm refers to joy, it's not speaking about a personality trait or temporary happiness. Rather, this joy is the result of being restored by God. Those who have this joy are like "those who dream." It's a joy so good that you think, *"I'm living the dream."* This is the joy God's people experienced when He brought them out of captivity and restored their fortunes.

What did their joy lead them to do?

"Then they said among the nations,
'The Lord has done great things for them.'
The Lord has done great things for us;
We are glad."

Joy is contagious! Regardless of your natural disposition or current circumstances, wouldn't you love to have a constant joy so evident that people around you say, *"I want whatever it is she has"*? This is the joy God brings.

Would others around you describe you as a joyful person? Why or why not?

"When the angels had left them and gone into heaven, the shepherds said to one another, 'Let's go to Bethlehem and see this thing that has happened, which the Lord has told us about.'
So they hurried off and found Mary and Joseph, and the baby, who was lying in the manger. When they had seen him, they spread the word concerning what had been told them about this child, and all who heard it were amazed at what the shepherds said to them."
—Luke 2:15-18

What the shepherds saw and heard on the first Christmas filled them with joy, and they couldn't keep the good news to themselves! They shared how God had made Himself known to them. And that's our calling too. We're called to share the ways God has shown Himself in our lives. Whether through sharing answers to prayers, encouraging others, or spreading joy, we, like the shepherds, are meant to tell the world about Emmanuel—God with us, born on Christmas morning.

Reread Psalm 126 below, and then turn this psalm into your own personal prayer:

"When the Lord gave me restoration,
I was like those who dream.
Then my mouth was filled with laughter,
and my tongue with shouts of joy;
then they said to one other,
'The Lord has done great things for her.'
The Lord has done great things for me;
I am glad.
Restore my heart to you, O Lord,
like streams in the desert!
Though I have seen tears,
I will find shouts of joy!
Though I have experienced weeping,
I will come home with shouts of joy,
bringing my blessings with me."

Conclude your time today allowing your heart to be filled with the joy of God's blessings. You are restored to your Maker and Creator, to the One true God who has blessed you with good things and loves you enough to be born in a manger and crucified on the cross. Rejoice and be glad, and share your joy with others!

Day 5: JOY – Jesus, Others, Yourself

Read: Psalm 16

For ten years, David was on the run from Saul, who was Israel's reigning king at the time. Saul, feeling threatened by David's popularity, tried to kill him several times. This psalm may have come to David's mind in the middle of a frightening situation when he felt he could be found and killed at any moment. Perhaps he was hiding in a cave or up in the branches of a tree while Saul's men searched below.

David's enemies were not ultimately Saul, the Philistines, or anyone else who threatened his life but Satan, who inspired these attacks. Satan is our enemy as well, seeking to steal our joy, peace, and even our lives. David couldn't run or hide, but he could pray to God: *"Keep me safe, God, for in you I take refuge."*

Have you ever started a prayer this way? In what ways can you relate to this passage? Jot down what comes to mind:

"You are my Lord." To take refuge in God, we must submit to Him as Lord. We each have to choose what we will seek: God, approval, admiration, money, or something else that brings us a sense of joy and security. David made the choice to follow God, making Him Lord of his life.

Where do you place your trust? In what ways does your sense of security come from something in this world (finances, relationships, success)?

_____

How can you "take refuge" in God?

"Not everyone who says to me, 'Lord, Lord,' will enter the kingdom of heaven, but only the one who does the will of my Father who is in heaven. Many will say to me on that day, 'Lord, Lord, did we not prophesy in your name and in your name drive out demons and in your name perform many miracles?' Then I will tell them plainly, 'I never knew you. Away from me, you evildoers!'"
—Matthew 7:21-23

Your decision to *"make Christ Lord"* doesn't change His status or yours—He is Lord whether people recognize it or not. But you can decide whether you will treat Him as Master and live accordingly. It's one thing to say, *"Lord, Lord."* It's another to live in agreement with these words.

"Lord, you alone are my portion and my cup."

We all know people who always want more, no matter how much they have. Perhaps we've been those people ourselves, hoping for more regardless of our current blessings. Unfortunately, this mindset breeds greed and discontentment. Some people go through their life being discontent. Some people go through life wishing away the present while dreaming of something better. But if you're not content with what God has given you now, you won't be content in the future either.

When you set your hope on anything other than God, two things can happen:

1. You won't get what you hope for, so you'll be discontent.
2. You will get what you hope for, but it won't satisfy, leaving you discontent.

In what situations are you most likely to fall into one of these categories?

"Lord, you alone are my portion and my cup;
you make my lot secure.
The boundary lines have fallen for me in pleasant places;
surely I have a delightful inheritance.
I will praise the Lord, who counsels me;
even at night my heart instructs me.
I keep my eyes always on the Lord.
With him at my right hand, I will not be shaken."

David knew he was blessed. A shepherd boy turned King of Israel, with promises of an eternal kingdom given to him and his descendants. But recognizing these blessings was a choice. Many people don't count their blessings and instead focus on their problems. Like David, you have much to be thankful for. Take some time now to thank God for a few of your blessings. Write them below:

The word *"JOY"* can be viewed as an acronym:

- "J" stands for *Jesus*
- "O" stands for *Others*
- "Y" stands for *Yourself*

When you put Jesus first and others before you, you experience true JOY, like David expresses here.

Are you experiencing this joy? Why or why not? How can you be more joyful? Ask God to give you this deep joy despite your circumstances.

Week 4: Love

Day 1: Be Made New in Love

Read: John 3:1-21

"Just as Moses lifted up the snake in the wilderness, so the Son of Man must be lifted up."

Now, read Numbers 21:4-9 below to understand the comparison Jesus makes between Himself and the bronze snake:

"They traveled from Mount Hor along the route to the Red Sea, to go around Edom. But the people grew impatient on the way; they spoke against God and against Moses, and said, 'Why have you brought us up out of Egypt to die in the wilderness? There is no bread! There is no water! And we detest this miserable food!'

Then the LORD sent venomous snakes among them; they bit the people and many Israelites died. The people came to Moses and said, 'We sinned when we spoke against the LORD and against you. Pray that the LORD will take the snakes away from us.' So Moses prayed for the people.

The LORD said to Moses, 'Make a snake and put it up on a pole; anyone who is bitten can look at it and live.' So Moses made a bronze snake and put it up on a pole. Then when anyone was bitten by a snake and looked at the bronze snake, they lived."
—Numbers 21:4-9

As we reflect on how Jesus is like the snake lifted up in the wilderness, there are key truths to consider about our need for new birth and how Jesus provides it.

---

1. All people are under the curse of death because of sin.
Whether the sin is grumbling against God, idolizing other things before Him, or struggles with pride, greed, lust, envy, or failing to love others as we should, we have all sinned more times than we can count. God cannot overlook sin and still be holy and just. And we cannot pay for our own sins, as we all fall short of God's glory.

2. God graciously provides the remedy for the curse.
Just as those bitten by snakes couldn't save themselves, we cannot rescue ourselves from sin.

It was only when the Israelites confessed their sin and sought Moses' intercession that God provided a remedy. Similarly, we're all condemned to death because of sin, with no human remedy available. But God graciously provided the remedy for our sin through His Son, lifted up in the wilderness.

3. The remedy must be lifted up.
The cross was essential to atone for our sins. There's a double meaning in "lifted up"—it also means to exalt or lift up in majesty. Just as the snake was lifted up to save the dying, Jesus was lifted up to save us. But God didn't leave Him on the cross; He raised Him from the dead and exalted Him in glory.

4. The only requirement for healing is to look in faith to God's remedy.

God could have removed the snakes, but instead, He provided a remedy that required nothing of the Israelites except faith to look upon it. Likewise, Jesus says, *"everyone who believes in Him will have eternal life."* Nothing else is required but faith. No amount of work or good deeds will bring salvation; it is a gift already given. All that's needed is trust and belief in Him.

How does Jesus' phrase "born again" align with your own experience of new birth?

"Therefore, if anyone is in Christ, the new creation has come: The old has gone, the new is here!"
—2 Corinthians 5:17

In what ways do you feel like a new creation since coming to know Christ?

What is new about your character, habits, or life since following Him?

How do you still need to allow God to shape and mold you? In what specific area(s) of your life do you need God to continue making you a new creation?

_____

What do you need to let go of to allow God to bring about these changes?

Read: Romans 6:6-12
"For we know that our old self was crucified with him so that the body ruled by sin might be done away with, that we should no longer be slaves to sin— because anyone who has died has been set free from sin. Now if we died with Christ, we believe that we will also live with him. For we know that since Christ was raised from the dead, he cannot die again; death no longer has mastery over him. The death he died, he died to sin once for all; but the life he lives, he lives to God."

"In the same way, count yourselves dead to sin but alive to God in Christ Jesus. Therefore do not let sin reign in your mortal body so that you obey its evil desires."

This week, be encouraged to remember that you are a new creation in Christ. There is hope in knowing you are no longer dead to sin but fully alive in Christ Jesus. As you encounter struggles, frustrations, or moments of overwhelm this week, pause, and ask Christ for His strength and power to live as a new creation.

Day 2: God is Love

Love is who God is. Love is part of His unchanging nature.

Read: Malachi 3:1, 3:6 & James 1:17

We can take great comfort in knowing that we serve a God who does not change. Theologians refer to this as the "immutability of God." God's nature, character, and love are unchanging.

"In the beginning you laid the foundations of the earth,
and the heavens are the work of your hands.
They will perish, but you remain;
they will all wear out like a garment.
Like clothing you will change them
and they will be discarded.
But you remain the same,
and your years will never end.
The children of your servants will live in your presence;
their descendants will be established before you."
—Psalm 102:25-28

"Jesus Christ is the same yesterday and today and forever."
—Hebrews 13:8

This claim in Hebrews is powerful, as only God is immutable—only He cannot and does not change. To say Jesus is the same yesterday, today, and forever is to affirm His deity. Who better to entrust our lives and salvation to than the one who is God and who does not change?

"I am the Alpha and the Omega," says the Lord God, "who is, and who was, and who is to come, the Almighty."
—*Revelation 1:8*

God's unchanging nature includes His attributes. Whatever qualities were His before the universe came into existence are still His now and will remain forever.

These attributes include:

- **He is trustworthy.** His purposes and promises are immutable.
  Read: Luke 4:16-27
- **His love is unchanging.**
  "Beloved, let us love one another, for love is from God, and whoever loves has been born of God and knows God. Anyone who does not love does not know God, because God is love. In this the love of God was made manifest among us, that God sent his only Son into the world, so that we might live through him. In this is love, not that we have loved God but that he loved us and sent his Son to be the propitiation for our sins."
  —*1 John 4:7-8*

"And so we know and rely on the love God has for us. God is love. Whoever lives in love lives in God, and God in them."
—*1 John 4:16*

"Though the mountains be shaken and the hills be removed, yet my unfailing love for you will not be shaken nor my covenant of peace be removed," says the Lord, who has compassion on you."
—*Isaiah 54:10*

"Give thanks to the God of heaven. His love endures forever!"
—*Psalm 136:26*

"But God demonstrates his own love for us in this: While we were still sinners, Christ died for us."
—*Romans 5:8*

The unchanging, everlasting God took on flesh and became man because of His great love for us. He wanted to restore our relationship with Him. Our salvation required a perfect sacrifice without blemish, and Jesus became that sacrifice for us.

Reflect on the depth of God's love through these truths:

- The King of Kings was once the child wrapped in cloths in a manger.
- He was the man arrested in the garden.
- He was the one without sin who hung on the cross.
- He was born to die for your sins, but He lived as a man to understand you and your weakness.

You can trust in the promises of God. You can trust in the love of God. May this trust bring you a joy and peace that surpasses understanding, overflows, and pours out to others.

Close your time in prayer. Where is God calling you to trust more? In what areas of your life would you benefit from reminders of all that is true about Him?

Day 3: Love Others Above Yourself

Read: 1 John 3:16-18

Love expressed through action is proof of its authenticity. Out of His deep love for us, our Heavenly Father acted on behalf of His children by sending His Son to earth to rescue us through His own sacrifice.

Read: 1 John 4:7-8 & James 1:22-25

We are called to love, just as Jesus did—through action. Jesus demonstrated His love in countless ways: healing, helping, washing feet, giving His time and attention, listening, and sacrificing.

What are some practical ways you can demonstrate love to others in your life? Consider a few specific examples:

Let's face it: some people are easier to love than others. For instance, it may feel natural to serve and sacrifice for our children, yet more challenging to extend the same love to others. Who are the people in your life that you find difficult to love, whether in your heart, words, or actions?

Read: Matthew 5:43-48

"Enemies" may sound like a strong word. You might think, *"But I have no enemies."* That may be true, and if so, the term could refer to those with whom you struggle to show love. "Enemy" is simply the opposite of "friend," so this may include anyone you don't hold close in your heart.

So, who are your "enemies"? How can you love them? What might that look like in action?

"And we ought to lay down our lives for our brothers and sisters." This doesn't mean laying down our lives in death as Christ did, but in everyday acts of love and service. Look at the next verse: *"If anyone has material possessions and sees a brother or sister in need but has no pity on them, how can the love of God be in that person?"* (1 John 3:17)

We are called to lay down our lives by serving others daily. This could mean sacrificing our time, sharing our resources, or surrendering personal rights for the good of others.

"You have heard that it was said, 'Love your neighbor and hate your enemy.' But I tell you, love your enemies and pray for those who persecute you, that you may be children of your Father in heaven. He causes his sun to rise on the evil and the good and sends rain on the righteous and the unrighteous. If you love those who love you, what reward will you get? Are not even the tax collectors doing that? And if you greet only your own people, what are you doing more than others?"
—*Matthew 5:43-47*

"Do nothing out of selfish ambition or vain conceit. Rather, in humility value others above yourselves, not looking to your own interests but each of you to the interests of the others."
—*Philippians 2:3-4*

We are called to a different kind of death—a death to our selfish nature. We're called to let go of the part of us that insists on being right, having our way, or seeking our own benefit.

Can you think of a time when God asked you to show love to someone you didn't particularly like, or to put someone else's needs before your own, even though it was challenging?

Ask God now to give you opportunities to show love through action, even to those you may consider "enemies" or difficult to love. Pray for the ability to express love, and ask God to fill you with His love, overflowing like a cup, so you can love as He has called you to love.

Day 4: Love as an Ambassador for Christ

Read: Luke 7:36-50

Thank goodness we have been forgiven much! Our many sins have been forgiven—and we can express great love and gratitude because of this. Forgiveness is an act of love. In His love for us, Jesus forgives our sins. Have you ever been called to love someone through forgiveness? Is there someone God might be calling you to love through forgiveness now?

Read: 2 Corinthians 5:14-21

Christ's sacrificial love compels us to action. It compels us to live and love for Him who died for us and was raised again. We are compelled because, as this passage tells us, we are new creations in Christ. Like new growth that blossoms in the spring, we blossom into a new creation as we bask in the love of the Father. "All this is from God, who reconciled us to himself through Christ."

"And when Jesus had cried out again in a loud voice, he gave up his spirit. At that moment the curtain of the temple was torn in two from top to bottom. The earth shook, the rocks split."
—Matthew 27:50-51

This verse describes the moment of our reconciliation with God. The temple curtain was torn from top to bottom. This curtain separated the Holy of Holies—the dwelling place of God's presence—from the rest of the temple. Only the high priest could enter this space once a year, on the day of atonement. But Jesus' sacrifice changed everything. The torn curtain symbolized the direct access all believers now have to God's presence.

"We are therefore Christ's ambassadors, as though God were making his appeal through us."
—2 Corinthians 5:20

What does it mean to be an ambassador?

- Ambassadors do not appoint themselves. As Christians, we are appointed by the Lord. You have been chosen by God to represent Him to others. To whom has God called you to represent Him in your life?

  "For we are God's handiwork, created in Christ Jesus to do good works, which God prepared in advance for us to do." –Ephesians 2:10

- An ambassador is fully supported by the one who appoints them. God provides everything you need to accomplish His work. Are you fully trusting that God will equip you to represent Him?

  "And this same God who takes care of me will supply all your needs from his glorious riches, which have been given to us in Christ Jesus." —Philippians 4:19

- An ambassador doesn't belong to the country to which he is sent. As Christians, we are citizens of Heaven. In what ways do you not feel like a citizen in this world - in today's culture?

"But we are citizens of heaven, where the Lord Jesus Christ lives. And we are eagerly waiting for him to return as our Savior." —Philippians 3:20

- An ambassador's purpose isn't for their own benefit, but to represent their homeland's interests. As Christ's ambassadors, we're called to serve others selflessly, seeking their good and honoring Christ through our humility.

"Who can know the Lord's thoughts? Who knows enough to teach him? But we understand these things, for we have the mind of Christ." —1 Corinthians 2:16

- An ambassador has written instructions. The Word of God is our guide.

"But don't just listen to God's word. You must do what it says. Otherwise, you are only fooling yourselves." —James 1:22

- Being an ambassador is the highest calling. Nothing is more significant than being used by God, and this is where we find true joy and fulfillment.

"I once thought these things were valuable, but now I consider them worthless because of what Christ has done. Yes, everything else is worthless when compared with the infinite value of knowing Christ Jesus my Lord." —Philippians 3:7-8

You are an ambassador for Christ, and there is no greater honor or privilege. Every conversation, interaction, word, and attitude is your chance to represent Christ Jesus and His love.

Reflect on Jesus' Call to You:

"Therefore go and make disciples of all nations, baptizing them in the name of the Father and of the Son and of the Holy Spirit, and teaching them to obey everything I have commanded you. And surely I am with you always, to the very end of the age."
—Matthew 28:19-20

May the overflowing love of Jesus fill you so completely that it pours out and blesses all who encounter you this Christmas season and beyond.

Day 5: Love Has Come

Read: Luke 1:67-79

In today's reading, we hear Zechariah reflect on the impact of Jesus' birth for the world. Words like *salvation*, *mercy*, *rescue*, *forgiveness*, and *peace* appear throughout this passage.

What does Jesus' birth mean to you personally? And what does it mean for the world around you today?

"to rescue us from the hand of our enemies,
and to enable us to serve him without fear
in holiness and righteousness before him all our days."
—Luke 1:74-75

Even today, there are countless things that can cause fear—heartbreak, sickness, loneliness, pain, betrayal, evil, and even a sense of meaninglessness. What particular fears would you like Jesus to free you from?

Christ's birth fulfills a promise made by God long ago, a testament to His unwavering faithfulness. Think about the times you've experienced God's promises fulfilled in your own life.

Where have you personally witnessed His faithfulness? Perhaps you've seen it through promises of hope, joy, forgiveness, strength, guidance, protection, provision, healing, peace, or unconditional love. Consider specific moments where God's faithfulness shone through in one of these areas, and reflect on how those promises have impacted your life.

Read: Romans 8:14-17

According to this passage, we hold privileges as children of God. What are some of these privileges? List as many as you can. How have you personally experienced these privileges in your life?

Tim Keller outlines seven privileges we have as children of God in his book *Romans 8-16 For You*. They are:

1. We have **security** in our relationship with the Father.
2. We have **authority** as God's children.
3. We can **cry out to our loving Father as "Abba"**, an intimate term for Father.
4. We have **assurance** through the Spirit that we are His.
5. As **heirs of God**, we have an inheritance.
6. We receive **discipline** from a Father who loves us.
7. We bear a **family likeness** as we share in Christ's sufferings.

Not all these "privileges" may immediately seem like privileges, yet they serve as proof that we are God's children. Which of these have you experienced recently?

_____

Jesus is God's ultimate gift, offered to all who choose to receive it. Have you ever had a special gift for someone, one you couldn't wait for them to open? Imagine how God feels about His gift of love, mercy, forgiveness, salvation, hope, and peace! Think of the Creator of the universe eagerly awaiting for all to receive His gift.

This Christmas, we are not only called to receive and behold Him. We are called to share Him.

May the blessings of God's gift fill you so fully that they overflow, touching everyone around you. May your heart be filled with hope, peace, joy, and love this season and always. Merry Christmas!

Bonus: A Holiday Devotional Leader Guide

Introduction

Leader Guide Contents

- **Welcome**
- **Using the Leader Guide**
- **Week 1**: Thanksgiving Devotionals
- **Week 2-4**: Christmas Devotionals
- **About the Author**

WELCOME

This Leader Guide is designed to help you facilitate meaningful discussions and foster deep connections within your small group as you journey through the holiday devotionals. These devotionals explore the themes of gratitude, joy, and love during the Thanksgiving and Christmas seasons, offering a rich opportunity to reflect on the blessings and hope we find in Christ.

"Do not conform to the pattern of this world, but be transformed by the renewing of your mind. Then you will be able to test and approve what God's will is — his good, pleasing, and perfect will." Romans 12:2

As we journey through this busy season, let this be a time to renew our minds and seek God's will above the world's distractions, focusing on what truly matters. May His good, pleasing, and perfect will shape our hearts and guide us in love, peace, and purpose.

Leading Your Holiday Devotionals Group

As you begin leading this holiday-themed small group, you'll guide members in discussions that focus on nurturing hearts of gratitude, finding joy in Christ, and spreading love during a season that can often feel rushed and hectic. This guide will provide the structure, support, and discussion questions needed to help your group connect, reflect, and grow together during this special time of year.

Getting Started

This guide includes sessions for one Thanksgiving-themed week and four Christmas-themed weeks. Begin your group by creating a welcoming space where participants feel comfortable sharing and reflecting. Each meeting focuses on themes from the devotionals, allowing time for group discussions and personal reflections. Your role as a leader will be to facilitate these discussions, encourage mutual support, and cultivate a spirit of unity and encouragement.

Using This Guide

Each session includes:

- **Opening Reflection:** Begin by inviting each group member to share something they're thankful for or to reflect on a theme from that week's devotionals.
- **Reading and Discussion:** Use the provided readings and questions in the Leader Guide to facilitate discussion on that week's Bible study from the devotionals. Each session includes selected passages and prompts to guide meaningful conversation, helping members connect personally with the week's devotionals and explore how they apply to their lives.
- **Personal Application:** Encourage members to reflect on how they can incorporate themes like gratitude, joy, and love into their daily lives, particularly during this holiday season.
- **Accountability Check-In (if applicable):** If your group is pairing the devotionals with the *Giving Thanks* and *12 Workouts of Christmas* programs from SoulStrength Fit, ask the accountability check-in questions before the closing prayer:
- **Closing Prayer:** Conclude by asking if there are any prayer requests, then pray together, focusing on gratitude, joy, and unity during this busy time of year.

Options for Group Study

Option 1: Using the Devotionals Alone

If your group is focusing solely on *Heartfelt Holidays: Devotionals for Thanksgiving & Christmas*, this guide provides a structured framework for a meaningful holiday-season study. Each session offers opportunities to reflect on selected devotional themes, share personal insights, and deepen your walk with God. This approach emphasizes building community, strengthening relationships, and fostering spiritual growth through the teachings and scriptures explored in the daily devotionals.

Option 2: Pairing with the SoulStrength Fit *Giving Thanks* and *12 Workouts of Christmas* Programs

For a fully integrated mind-body-spirit experience, consider pairing the devotionals with SoulStrength Fit's *Giving Thanks* and *12 Workouts of Christmas* programs. This option enhances the group experience by combining faith-based workouts with Bible study and spiritual reflection, supporting growth in both physical health and spiritual well-being. Each program includes three weekly faith-based workouts corresponding with the devotionals, offering a unique way to worship through exercise.

This Leader Guide equips you to facilitate weekly sessions where members can come together for spiritual encouragement, accountability, and fellowship. By pairing the devotionals with the workout programs, your group can experience a powerful, integrated journey that strengthens both body and spirit throughout the holiday season. Learn more and sign up for these programs at www.soulstrengthfit.com.

Tips for Leading Your Holiday Group

Creating a warm, supportive environment is essential for your small group this holiday season. The goal is to help everyone feel comfortable sharing, reflecting, and encouraging one another as you journey through Heartfelt Holidays together. Start by uplifting and supporting each member, especially in this busy season.

Encourage group interaction by fostering a welcoming atmosphere where everyone feels free to share experiences, reflections, and any tips for staying centered during this time of year. Ask questions with genuine interest and warmth, and listen carefully to each response. Remember, the heart of this group lies in the process and shared moments, not in finding specific answers.

As a leader, guide conversations with flexibility. Feel free to rephrase questions from the Leader Guide to suit your group's needs, and adjust time spent on various topics to allow for meaningful discussion. You have the option to skip or add questions as needed. Ensure that no one person, including yourself, dominates the conversation, and gently redirect if necessary. Allow each person to participate at their own comfort level; not everyone needs to answer every question, and it's okay if some members take time to open up.

If questions arise that you don't have answers for, it's perfectly fine to say, "I'm not sure about that one, but I'll look into it." This approach invites collaborative learning and encourages group engagement. Embrace the season's spirit by being open, kind, and flexible, letting God guide you in your role as a leader.

The Heart of Thanksgiving
1 Week Leader Guide

Heart of Thanksgiving: A Week of Grateful Reflection

Opening Prayer

Begin your session with a short prayer, inviting God's presence and thanking Him for the opportunity to gather. Ask for hearts that are open to gratitude, reflection, and encouragement during this time.

Opening Reflection

Question:

Let's begin by sharing three things we are each grateful for. Name three blessings in your life or the ways in which God has been faithful.

Gratitude and Ingratitude

Read: Colossians 3:12-17

Question:

One common struggle we may share is ingratitude. With so much at our disposal, we often lose our sense of gratitude and dependence on God. Ingratitude can hinder our generosity toward others, whether financially, through patience, forgiveness, compassion, or Christ-like love. It also robs us of humility and brings a sense of dissatisfaction into our lives.

What's an area of your life in which you are most likely to struggle with ingratitude, and how does that ingratitude negatively affect your heart of generosity, humility, or gratitude?

Reflecting on Colossians 3:12-17

Question:

Colossians describes characteristics that believers are called to embody. Which of these characteristics do you find most challenging to embody or need to focus on more in your daily life?

Fears that Affect Us

Reflect on the role of fear in your life. Fear can often cloud our sense of gratitude and peace.

Here are four common fears:

- The fear of loss – Fear of losing family, marriage, finances, or health.
- The fear of failure – Fear that holds us back from trying new things or setting meaningful goals.
- The fear of rejection – Fear of forming new relationships or feeling truly seen.
- The fear of the unknown – A dread of future uncertainties or what could go wrong.

Question:

Which of these fears resonates with you most, and how does it show up in your life?

Finding Comfort in God

Read: 2 Corinthians 1:3-4

Question:

Think about a "storm" you have faced or are currently facing. How might God be calling you to use the comfort you've received in this situation to encourage or support others who may be going through something similar?

Optional Reflection:

Alternatively, think of a time when you received comfort from someone who had endured a similar storm. How did their support impact you, and how does it inspire you to support others?

Battling Expectations

Question:

Do you find yourself struggling to live up to certain expectations—whether from others, from yourself, or from what you feel God expects? Which of these—others' expectations, self-imposed standards, or expectations you feel come from God—do you find yourself struggling with the most? How does this affect your ability to show yourself grace when you fall short?

Responses to the Pressure of Expectations

Question:

We often respond to pressure in different ways:

- Sustaining a False Image – Striving to maintain a certain image, even if it's not fully true.

- Avoiding Risks or Challenges – Holding back out of fear it won't meet high standards.
- Obsessing Over Details – Fixating on getting things "just right," sometimes to the point of ineffectiveness.

Which of these responses resonates most with you? How does it tend to show up in your life, and

how might it affect your ability to show grace to yourself?

Letting Go of Perfectionism

Read: Luke 10:38-42

Question:

Reflect on Jesus' words to Martha, "My dear Martha, you are worried and upset over all these details! There is only one thing worth being concerned about. Mary has discovered it, and it will not be taken away from her."

As you consider the upcoming holiday season, how might your experience look different if you let go of perfectionism, choosing to prioritize relationships over appearances and true connection above trying to get everything "just right"? What specific changes might you make to experience the season more fully and with greater peace?

Accountability Check-In (if pairing with the SoulStrength Fit Workout Program):

- Did you complete your workouts this week? What helped you stay on track, or what challenges made it difficult?
- How did you feel about your nutrition and eating habits this week? Share a specific example of a day when you felt aligned with your goals or a time when it was challenging to stay on track.

Closing Prayer

Conclude by asking if there are any specific prayer requests, then close in prayer. Focus on themes of gratitude, humility, and joy, and ask for strength in letting go of fears, unrealistic expectations, and perfectionism as you each strive to live fully and gratefully in God's presence this season.

The Heart of
Christmas
Leader Guide

Week 1: Hope

Opening Prayer

Begin your session by inviting God's presence. Ask for hearts open to experiencing peace, hope, and connection to Christ as you begin this journey into the Christmas season. Pray for wisdom and encouragement as you prepare to celebrate the birth of Jesus.

Opening Reflection

Question:

The holiday season often becomes a whirlwind of activity—shopping, wrapping gifts, baking, and decorating. In the midst of all this, how are we preparing spiritually?
Consider the emotions and challenges you typically encounter during the holidays, such as feeling overwhelmed, lonely, or exhausted. Now, think about what you would like to experience this Christmas. How would you like to feel, and what would a spiritually fulfilling holiday season look like for you?

God's Promises in Waiting
Read: Micah 5:2-4 & Matthew 2:1-6

Question:

These passages remind us that God fulfills His promises, even when it feels like He's silent. Can you think of a time when you felt like you were waiting on a promise from God, or perhaps you feel you're in a season of waiting right now? Has there been a time when God seemed silent, but looking back, you can see how He was at work? What life experiences come to mind when you think about waiting on the Lord to fulfill a promise or to take action after a period of waiting?

Perfect Timing and Purposeful Waiting
Read: Galatians 4:4-6

Question:

In this passage, Paul says, "when the time came to completion, God sent his Son…" What do you think it means for the time to come to completion? Reflecting on your own life, is there an area where you're currently waiting on the Lord, praying for change, or seeking an answer?
Consider the quote, *"God is always doing 10,000 things in your life, and you may only be aware of three of them."* How might God be working behind the scenes—preparing your heart, refining your character, or shaping circumstances—so that His perfect timing can unfold? How could this waiting season be part of God's plan for your future?

Reflecting on the Names of Jesus

Read: Isaiah 9:6

Questions:

Isaiah 9:6 gives us four powerful names for Jesus: *Wonderful Counselor, Mighty God, Eternal Father,* and *Prince of Peace.* Take a moment to consider each name and how Jesus lived out these roles during His ministry on earth.

- How did Jesus fulfill each of these roles as described in this verse during His time on earth?
- How does He personally fulfill these names in your life?
- Which of these names resonates most strongly with you in this season of life? How so?

Accountability Check-In (if pairing with the SoulStrength Fit Workout Program):

- Did you complete your workouts this week? What helped you stay on track, or what challenges made it difficult?
- How did you feel about your nutrition and eating habits this week? Share a specific example of a day when you felt aligned with your goals or a time when it was challenging to stay on track.

Closing Prayer

End your time by gathering prayer requests and praying together. Ask for grace, patience, and a focus on Christ as you navigate the busyness of the season. Pray that each person would experience God's peace, joy, and assurance as they await His promises and reflect on the true meaning of Christmas.

Week 2: Peace & Preparation

Opening Prayer

Begin your session by inviting God's presence. Pray for open hearts as you explore the theme of peace this week. Ask for grace to release any anxieties and to find rest in God's promises, especially during the holiday season.

Opening Reflection

Question:

As you enter the Christmas season, take a moment to consider your hopes for this time. Beyond the activities and traditions, what are your personal intentions for the season? Are there qualities— like peace, gratitude, or joy—you'd like to cultivate more deeply?

Question:

If you could capture the spirit of what you hope for this holiday season in a few words, what would they be?

The Heart of the Holiday Season: A Mary or Martha Approach?

111

Read: Luke 10:38-42

Question:

Consider the times during the holiday season when you tend to act more like Martha. What situations or tasks bring out that "Martha" mindset in you? How does this affect your attitude, your sense of joy, or your ability to be present and enjoy the moment?

Finding Peace Beyond Our Problems

"…and on earth peace to those on whom his favor rests." (Luke 2:14)

God's favor rests on you, and He offers you His peace. Yet, when we doubt this peace—or fail to feel it—it's often because we're trying to manage life's challenges in our own strength. The peace we seek is often a solution to our problems, rather than a quiet heart in the midst of them.

Question: In which areas of your life are you currently missing out on God's peace because you're trying to handle or fix the situation yourself? How might seeking a quiet heart, rather than immediate answers, change your approach?

Understanding True Peace

Read: Ephesians 2:11-18

Question:

Reflecting on this passage, consider: What do you think is the difference between having peace with God and simply feeling peaceful? Are both always present together? Why or why not? In what areas of your life do you feel a sense of peace with God, yet often struggle to feel calm, peaceful, or at ease?

Trusting in God's Promises

Read: Luke 1:30-38

In this passage, Gabriel reassures Mary, who is understandably frightened by his greeting, telling her in verse 30, "Do not be afraid, Mary; you have found favor with God." He doesn't stop there—he goes on to remind her of an important truth in verse 37: "For no word from God will ever fail."

God gives us many promises in His Word, including promises of protection, guidance, forgiveness, hope, strength, eternal life, provision, comfort, peace, unconditional love, presence, wisdom, healing, joy, justice, mercy, victory over sin, answered prayer, new life, restoration, faithfulness, and abundant life.

Question:

Which of God's promises would you benefit most from trusting in right now? How would leaning into this promise impact your faith or bring you peace in your current circumstances?

Receiving Jesus' Gift of Peace

Read: John 14:27

In this verse, Jesus promises His disciples the gift of peace, assuring them—and us—not to be afraid or anxious. He offers you this same peace today.

Question:

What fears, worries, or anxieties could you bring before the Lord to experience this gift of peace more fully? How might trusting in Jesus' promise of peace help you let go of specific anxieties and deepen your sense of calm?

Accountability Check-In (if pairing with the SoulStrength Fit Workout Program):

Did you complete your workouts this week? What helped you stay on track, or what challenges made it difficult?
How did you feel about your nutrition and eating habits this week? Share a specific example of a day when you felt aligned with your goals or a time when it was challenging to stay on track.

Closing Prayer

End by gathering prayer requests and praying together. Ask for hearts that are open to Christ's peace and promises, especially during this busy season. Pray for each member to experience a quiet heart and to let go of any anxieties, finding rest in God's presence as they seek His peace.

Week 3: Joy

Opening Prayer

Begin your session by inviting God's presence and asking for hearts open to the joy of the season. Pray that each person would encounter the true joy that comes from knowing and sharing Christ. Ask for God's guidance in living out His joy through humble service, trust in Him, and a focus on Jesus above all else.

Opening Reflection

Question:

Let's start by reflecting on what brings us joy. Think of one experience, person, or memory that filled you with genuine joy. How might we seek this kind of joy in our relationship with Christ this season?

Boldly Sharing God's Word and Bringing Joy to Others
Read: Acts 13:42-52

Sharing God's Message

Question:

Paul and Barnabas boldly shared the gospel despite facing strong opposition, trusting that God could use them to spread His word. Reflecting on this, in what ways do you feel God might be calling you to share His message with others? Consider the unique opportunities in your life—your relationships, workplace, or community—where you might reflect His truth and love. How could God use you to share His message with those around you?

Being a Source of Joy

Question:
Paul and Barnabas experienced joy even in the face of rejection, knowing they were fulfilling God's call. Joy can come not only from sharing the gospel but also through acts of kindness, encouragement, and love. How might God be calling you to bring joy to others, whether through sharing His word or through your actions? Think of 3-5 specific ways you could bring His light and joy to those around you.

Guided Reflection on Psalm 23: The Lord as Our Shepherd

Read: Psalm 23

Questions:

The Lord's Protection
Can you recall a specific time when the Lord protected you, either physically or emotionally? How did you recognize His protection in that situation?

The Lord's Guidance
Think of a particular moment when you felt guided by God's wisdom or direction. How did He lead you, and what difference did it make in your life?

The Lord's Comfort in Times of Uncertainty
Reflect on a season of challenge or uncertainty—can you identify a way that the Lord provided comfort or reassurance during that time? How did His presence bring peace or strength to you?

Loving Humbly and Serving Others

Read: John 13:1-17

Everyday Acts of Humble Service
In this passage, Jesus demonstrates profound humility by washing His disciples' feet, a gesture of love and service. What are some everyday examples in your life that might be equivalent to washing feet? Consider acts of service, kindness, or humility that mirror Jesus' example.

Struggling to Follow Jesus' Example

In what situations do you struggle to humbly love and serve as Jesus would if He were in your shoes? What makes it difficult for you to take on a servant's heart in these situations?

Loving Humbly in Your Relationships

Who is God calling you to love more humbly right now? Think of specific relationships where you could offer more patience, compassion, or a spirit of service. How might following Jesus' example of humility impact these relationships?

Finding Our Security in God

Read: Psalm 16:1-2

"Keep me safe, my God, for in you I take refuge. I say to the Lord, 'You are my Lord; apart from you I have no good thing.'"

Choosing Where to Place Our Trust

Question:

Reflecting on this passage, we each have to decide what we seek for our joy and security: God, approval, admiration, success, or something else. Where do you place your trust most often? In what ways are you tempted to find security in things of this world, such as finances, relationships, approval, or achievements?

Finding Refuge in God Alone

Question:

How would shifting your trust fully to God change your perspective on these worldly sources of security? Consider how God's promise of refuge and safety might reshape your outlook on the things you're most tempted to rely on.

Living Out True JOY

The word "JOY" can serve as an acronym to remind us of how to approach life's challenges and keep our priorities in balance:

- "J" stands for *Jesus*
- "O" stands for *Others*
- "Y" stands for *Yourself*

Question:

Consider a current challenge or problem you are facing. How might applying the "JOY" acronym—putting Jesus first, others second, and yourself last—bring purpose, peace, or a new perspective to this situation? What changes might this approach inspire in your attitude or actions?

Accountability Check-In (if pairing with the SoulStrength Fit Workout Program):

- How did your workouts go this week? What helped you stay on track, or what challenges did you encounter?
- Reflect on your nutrition and eating habits this week. Can you share an example of when you felt aligned with your goals or a time that was challenging?

Closing Prayer

Conclude by gathering any specific prayer requests. Pray together, asking God to fill each person with His joy and peace, guiding them in trusting Him above all else. Ask for hearts open to humbly serve, boldly share His love, and find joy through Christ in every aspect of the holiday season. Pray that each person would be a light and source of joy to others around them.

Week 4: Love

Opening Prayer

Begin the session by inviting God's presence and praying for open hearts that reflect Christ's love. Ask that each person may be filled with gratitude for His love and strengthened to show this love to others in meaningful, transformative ways. Pray for the Holy Spirit's guidance as you explore what it means to live as new creations in Christ and ambassadors of His love.

Becoming a New Creation

Read: 2 Corinthians 5:17
"Therefore, if anyone is in Christ, the new creation has come: The old has gone, the new is here!"

Reflection on Transformation
Reflecting on our new identity in Christ can reveal areas of growth and invite deeper transformation.

Questions:

- How do you feel like a new creation since coming to know Christ? What is new about your character, habits, or life since following Him?
- In what areas of your life do you still need to allow God to shape and mold you? Are there specific areas where He is calling you to grow or change?

- What do you need to let go of to fully embrace these changes and allow God to make you into the person He has called you to be?

———————

Demonstrating Love in Action
Read: 1 John 3:16-18

Question:

We are called to love as Jesus did, not only through words but through meaningful actions. Jesus showed His love in practical ways: by healing, helping, listening, giving time, washing feet, and ultimately through His sacrifice.

What are some practical ways you can demonstrate love to others in your life? Consider specific examples where you might show active, Christ-like love in your daily life.

Loving Those Who Are Hard to Love
Read: Matthew 5:43-48

Question:

Jesus calls us to extend love even to those who are difficult to love, those we may not hold close in our hearts.

Who are the "enemies" or challenging people in your life? How might you show love to them, and what would that look like in action? Consider practical steps to demonstrate Christ-like love in these relationships.

Living as Christ's Ambassador

Read: 2 Corinthians 5:20, Ephesians 2:10

Questions:
As Christ's ambassadors, we are chosen and appointed by God to represent Him, assured that He provides all we need to fulfill this role.

- In this season of life, what does it look like for you to be an ambassador of Christ? Who are the specific people or groups God is calling you to reach or serve, and how might you live out this role in your daily interactions?
- Consider the assurance that God provides everything you need to accomplish His work. How confident do you feel in trusting that He will supply what you need to fulfill this role as His ambassador?

Freedom from Fear Through Christ

Read: Luke 1:67-75

Question:
In Zechariah's prophecy, Jesus is coming to free us from fear, enabling us to serve God without fear and to live in holiness and righteousness.

Even today, there are countless things that can cause fear—heartbreak, sickness, loneliness, pain, betrayal, evil, and even a sense of meaninglessness. Take a moment to consider a specific fear that you'd like to let go of this season. What would it look like to hand this fear over to Jesus, trusting Him to bring you peace and freedom? How might living in God's peace and freedom from this fear change your daily life?

The Ultimate Gift: Receiving and Sharing God's Blessings

As we conclude this journey, remember that God has given us the ultimate gift—eternal salvation through Jesus Christ. His gift transforms not only our eternal destiny but our lives here and now.

As Psalm 27:13 reminds us, *"I remain confident of this: I will see the goodness of the Lord in the land of the living."* God desires for us to experience a joy-filled, peace-saturated, purpose-driven life, reflecting His love in all we do.

Just as we cherish giving gifts to those we love, imagine how God must feel as He waits for each of us to unwrap His perfect gift— filled with love, mercy, forgiveness, salvation, hope, and peace. This Christmas, we are called not only to receive and behold this gift for ourselves but to share it with others.

May God's gift fill you to overflowing, so that His hope, peace, joy, and love shine brightly through you, touching everyone around you. Embrace His blessings and pass them on to others.

Accountability Check-In (if pairing with the SoulStrength Fit Workout Program)

- Did you complete your workouts this week? What helped you stay on track, or what challenges made it difficult?
- How did you feel about your nutrition and eating habits this week? Share a specific example of a day when you felt aligned with your goals or a time when it was challenging to stay on track.

Closing Prayer

Close by gathering any prayer requests, and then pray for hearts filled with Christ's love. Ask for the strength to live as His ambassadors, representing Him with courage and joy. Pray for His peace to overcome any fear and for His love to overflow, touching everyone you meet. May this season of reflection deepen your relationship with Christ and inspire you to share His love abundantly.

About the Author

Kelly Wenner is the founder and creator of SoulStrength Fit and SoulStrength Fit Kids and hosts the podcast *Devotionals on the Go*. With a background in faith-based fitness and devotionals, Kelly is dedicated to helping others grow spiritually, honor God with their lives, and nurture both their physical and spiritual health. Her mission is to empower people to realize their God-given potential, deepening their faith and discovering how to live vibrant, purpose-driven lives in alignment with God's will.

Kelly believes everyone can experience the fullness of God's peace and joy—not only during the holiday season but throughout every season of life. She prays that through this book, readers will find encouragement and inspiration to embrace God's love, share it with others, and reflect His light and hope in a world that deeply needs it.